My Beauty

a guide to looking & feeling great

Other books by Marlene Wallach

My Life:
A Guide to Health & Fitness

My Look:
A Guide to Fashion & Style

My Self:
A Guide to Me

marlene wallach

president, wilhelmina kids & teens modeling agency

WITH GRACE NORWICH

My Beauty

a guide to looking & feeling great

Aladdin

NEW YORK   LONDON   TORONTO   SYDNEY

ALADDIN

An imprint of Simon & Schuster Children's Publishing Division

1230 Avenue of the Americas, New York, NY 10020

Designed by Karin Paprocki

The text of this book was set in ITC Avant Garde Gothic.

Manufactured in China

First Aladdin edition August 2009

2 4 6 8 10 9 7 5 3 1

Library of Congress Control Number 2008938692

ISBN: 978-1-4169-7909-8

To my sister, Maxine,
who always helped me with the challenges
of growing up. Everyone always said
she was the beautiful, smart one
and I was the outgoing, popular one.

CONTENTS

a note
FROM MARLENE

THESE BOOKS ARE ALL ABOUT YOU AND your unique beauty. They're about letting others see the really incredible person you are. *My Beauty* focuses on physical beauty and the part of you that other people can see.

"Beauty is in the eye of the beholder." You've probably heard that expression before, but what does it mean? It means that the person doing the looking is the one who decides what's beautiful. It also means that not everyone sees beauty in the same way. This book will help you find your own kind of beauty.

When it comes to feeling good about your appearance, it's important to make the most of what's unique about you. I wish someone had told me that when it came to my curly hair. When I was younger, straight hair was the only style that was popular, and I did everything I could to get rid of what I now know is one of the strongest attributes of my look—my curly hair. Now it's your turn to learn to love and take care of all the great things that are part of you.

From my years in the beauty business, I can't stress enough how important it is to maintain healthy hair, skin, nails, and teeth. They are essential to looking your best. For models, it's an everyday part of the job. It may take some time for you to achieve flawless skin, glossy hair, and strong, lustrous nails, but it doesn't have to be a full-time job. I can help you make your beauty regimen fun, fast, and effective.

My Beauty is all about effortlessly looking and feeling great so you have more time to spend with friends, do your schoolwork, or play sports. With essential tips and easy-to-follow guidelines, you'll have everything you need to feel self-confident and free to express yourself and be who you are. In this book, you will find styles and products that will work for you—from the right haircut for the shape of your face, to the right braces for your teeth, to the perfect fragrance for making you feel special. When it comes to beauty, one size does not fit all. You will get the secrets you need for your personal dazzle to shine from the inside out. *My Beauty* is your resource to pick up and refer to over and over. So let's not waste another second—we've got some fun and exciting work to do!

chapter 1

HAIR AND MAKEUP

WHEN A MODEL ARRIVES AT A photo shoot, her first stop is "hair and makeup." She needs to have the professional touch before she's ready to step in front of the camera. Hair and makeup are the basis of a model's entire look and will complement the clothes she will be wearing. If her hair isn't right or if she has too much makeup on, the most beautiful dress in the world isn't going to look like the one you want to grab off the hanger. So let's talk about hair first. Here's a primer on how to get lovely locks that would make even Rapunzel jealous.

SALON READY

F YOU ARE LIKE MOST KIDS, YOUR MOM has been cutting your hair ever since you had enough hair on your head to cut. If you haven't already done so, at some point soon you'll be ready to head to the salon (maybe when you've saved up enough allowance!). Here's what you need to know to get the most out of your trip to a hairstylist.

Find the Right Salon

IT CAN BE HARD TO FIGURE OUT THE RIGHT place to get your hair cut. A salon might have pictures of gorgeous models gracing its storefront window, but in reality, that doesn't mean a thing. A great way to find the salon that works for you is to ask around. When you see someone with a great haircut, ask which salon they went to. Call the salon and make sure it's in your price range before you book an appointment.

Find a Haircut You Like

START LOOKING IN MAGAZINES FOR HAIR-

styles you like that will complement your natural beauty. The

saying "A picture is worth a thousand words" is especially true

when it comes to getting a haircut. It's much easier to show a

stylist a picture of what you want than it is to try to describe it.

What Shape Is Your Face?

FIGURING OUT THE SHAPE OF YOUR FACE

will help you find the right haircut. Here's how you do it.

You'll need a tape measure, paper, and a pen or pencil.

1. Measure the width of your face at the top of your cheekbones and write it down.
2. Measure the width of your face at the jaw and write
   that down.
3. Do the same thing just above your eyebrow line.
4. Measure your face from your hairline to your chin.
5. Match your results to one of the types below and discover
   what haircut will look best with your face.

hairline

eyebrow-line

cheekbones

jaw

chin

Haircuts for Different Shapes

NOW THAT YOU KNOW THE SHAPE OF YOUR

face, check out which cuts suit you best.

ROUND

The length and width of your face are about equal. Your face

is cute as a button. To show it off, opt for longer styles that

8

offset your round face. Don't go for a cut that's shorter than chin length. Updos and ponytails are particularly flattering—especially if you have some layers around your face. Light bangs work great on round faces as well.

OVAL

The length of your face is about one and a half times longer than the width. You've won the jackpot with this face! You can wear short or long haircuts, since lots of styles look good with an oval face. Try a cut with layers near your cheekbones, lips, or chin for the best look. The layers will draw attention to whichever gorgeous feature you want to highlight.

SQUARE

Your forehead and jawline are about equal in width. Your face is as strong as your personality. Go for heavy bangs or center parts. Curls or choppy layers are the perfect fit for a square face. Long hair with layers that start at the jaw and continue downward is another good choice. Avoid chin-length cuts.

HEART

The widths across your forehead and cheekbones are the widest, while your jawline is narrow. What's not to love about a heart-shaped face? Opt for either a bob or long hair. Avoid a shoulder-length cut that may make your chin look too pointy. Try soft layers around your fabulous cheekbones.

STYLE FILE

So MANY HAIRSTYLES, SO LITTLE time. In order to get the right look for your locks, it's important to know yourself. Are you a wash-and-go girl, or do you wield a blow dryer like a samurai? It's also important to know your hair type. Here's how to find the right hairstyle for you.

Styling Tips for Different Hair Types

STICK STRAIGHT

First, squeeze the excess moisture out of your hair after you wash it. Next, divide your hair into sections and apply a little straightening serum or pomade for some extra shine. To keep it all organized, take a big clip and clip the sections while you work on them one at a time. Pull down the section you're working on with a flat brush and blow dry, aiming the nozzle of the blow dryer down as well. This will help minimize frizzies.

My Notes

Now that you're an expert on face shapes, you can help your friends and classmates determine their face shapes and the haircuts that would suit them best.

CRAZY CURLY

The most important thing to remember about curls is to let them do their own thing after they've been washed. Brush out your hair right before you get into the shower. Use conditioner as part of your regular shampooing routine, since

curly hair tends to be dry. After washing, do not comb or brush your locks. Simply scrunch your hair with your fingers and apply a curl styling cream for added hydration and style control. Lastly, twirl one-inch sections around your finger if you want to make ringlets. Let those curls air dry, then spend that extra time thanking your lucky stars that your hair is so easy—wash and wear.

Memo from Marlene

My best curly hair day was when I got caught in the rain. I came back inside and my hair dried naturally. It looked fabulous! Rainwater—who would have thought that would be the secret ingredient?

WONDERFULLY WAVY

Fight frizz with a hydrating shampoo and conditioner. Look for shea butter. Shea butter, the natural fat extracted from the fruit of shea trees, is a rich moisturizer used in many cosmetic products. After squeezing out the extra moisture from your hair, apply a dollop of curl-sculpting cream. Divide your hair into four sections and style each one separately, scrunching

13

up the hair while you blow-dry it. A diffuser attachment is a good tool to add to your blow dryer, since it blows hot air indirectly, which keeps it from flattening waves. Soon you'll have waves as big and beautiful as the ocean.

Don't Be a Hothead

Follow these rules and you won't get fried by your blow dryer.

- To save time and energy, start blow-drying your hair only after you've squeezed out any excess moisture.
- Use an ionic hair dryer. It dries hair faster because the ionic energy breaks down the water molecules in your wet hair.
- Always keep the dryer moving, so you don't heat any one spot too much.
- Make sure the hair dryer is no less than six inches from your head.
- Use your diffuser: The plastic

My Notes
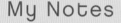
To speed up the styling process, try a stylist's secret: After you squeeze out all the excess water, blow-dry your hair until it is almost dry, then start to style, and the process will go much more quickly.

attachment in the shape of a bell that fits onto the nozzle of your blow dryer minimizes heat damage by sending the heat evenly through your hair. Diffusers also come in the shape of a small tube that flares out at the end. This is for drying and styling a more defined area. You have to keep the diffuser close to the hair, since the flow of air coming through it is indirect and cooler than that of a blow dryer.

Hairdos as Simple as 1, 2, 3

THE PERFECT PONY

Step 1: Apply a dollop of smoothing serum to your hair.

Step 2: Tilt your head back forty-five degrees and run a brush through your hair.

Step 3: Position the ponytail about two inches from the nape of your neck, tie it off with an elastic band, and finish by smoothing flyaways with your hands.

THE BEST BRAID

Step 1: Divide your hair into two equal sections and tie one off with an elastic band.

Step 2: Take the loose hair and divide it into three sections.

Step 3: First, cross the section in your left hand over the center piece of hair, then cross the section in your right hand over

the center piece. Continue braiding tightly until you have an inch of hair left. Then tie off the end with an elastic band and repeat on the other side.

THE MOST BEAUTIFUL BUN

Step 1: Brush your hair back into a low ponytail.

Step 2: Take the end of your ponytail and coil it around the elastic band, tucking the end of the pony into the bun.

Step 3: Hold the bun in place while you use bobby pins or hairpins around the edge of the bun to secure it to your head.

17

RED CARPET GLAMOUR

D ID YOU EVER WONDER HOW CELEBS get their hair to look a certain way? Once you learn the simple tricks behind these celebrity styles, people will be asking for *your* autograph.

Alluring Waves

THIS IS ONE OF THE EASIEST DOS, AND IT WILL have your friends thinking you spent hours with a curling iron.

- Mist your hair with water to make it slightly damp before bed.
- Make several big braids.
- In the morning, undo the braids and unleash those waves!

Braid Halo

HERE A SIMPLE BRAID BECOMES A HEAD-band for a very romantic look. Your hair needs to be longer than shoulder length for this one.

18

- Take a one-inch section of hair from behind your ear and create a tight braid on the side of your head.
- Pull the braid up and lay it over your head like a headband.
- Pin the end behind your other ear.
- Pull out wisps of hair around your face to add a romantic touch.

Memo from Marlene

Never cut your bangs when they're wet. You have no idea how much they'll "shrink up" when they dry, and they can turn out to be much shorter than you'd like. If you've done the damage and they're too short, wet your hair, put hair gel on your fingertip, pull your bangs over to the side, spreading the gel, and use a bobby pin to secure them near your temple. Tucked back, they'll practically disappear while they're growing out.

Flower Power

FRESH OR SILK FLOWERS ARE A TERRIFIC addition to any hairstyle. Try this one out for starters.

- Gather your hair into a low ponytail at the nape of your neck and secure it with an elastic band.

- Clip a flower onto the elastic, positioning it slightly off center so it'll be noticeable from either side.

Cheat Sheet!

MOST PEOPLE PART THEIR HAIR ON the same side every day. If you want dramatic, model-like hair for a special occasion, switch your part to the other side. You will be amazed at how much fuller and bouncier your hair becomes.

Glam Galore

FOR THE SIMPLE, CAREFREE LOOSE WAVES

you see on the runway, give this one a try. It requires a curling iron, so be sure to have adult supervision.

- Wrap three-inch sections of your hair around the barrel of a curling iron. You will be curling the bottom part of your hair only.
- Make certain the ends are fully wrapped, clamp down, and hold for seven full seconds.
- Open the iron and let the hair fall into your palm until it cools down.
- Holding the bottle ten inches or so from your hair, spray on gel.

Memo from Marlene

Hairstyling can get really pricey, but have no fear, a free haircut's near! You'd be surprised how many salons have these deals. And don't worry—there's always a teacher on hand to make sure the student stylist stays on track.

FEED YOUR HEAD AND YOUR HAIR: RULES FOR HEALTHY HAIR

Getting to the Root

BEFORE YOU BUY A SINGLE PRODUCT OR turn on that tap to wash your hair, consider that nutrition has a major impact on the way you look. What you eat has more effect on the health of your hair than any shampoo you can buy. Vitamins are what give hair its pretty sheen and texture. There is some controversy about which vitamins play the greatest role when it comes to your hair—is it vitamin E, or B vitamins, or omega-3 fatty acids?—so be sure to take a daily multivitamin to help ensure the right balance. There are lots of naturally occurring vitamins in a good diet, so make sure you eat plenty of fresh fruit, veggies, whole grains, and protein, such as dairy, meat, fish, or nuts.

Wash and Wear

YOU DO NOT NEED TO WASH YOUR HAIR

every night, unless it's very fine or gets oily quickly. It's best to

wash it three times a week or when it gets dirty after swimming

or playing sports. No matter how often

you need to wash your hair, use

a small amount of shampoo,

because it can dry out

your hair over time. All

you need is a dollop

the size of a quarter.

Rub the shampoo into

the roots of your hair and

rinse. Voilà!—that's all it takes.

Memo from Marlene

Young models often ask me how many times a day they should brush their hair. You'll probably want to brush your hair: (1) when you wake up, (2) when you get home from school or after-school activities, and (3) before bed.

Help for Common Hair Woes

TANGLE TAMERS

Tangles are truly a nuisance. Not only does it hurt when you

or your mom comb them out, but the process of running a

comb through tangles can damage your hair. Stop tangles in

their tracks by brushing your hair before you wash it or before you go to sleep. After showering, squeeze the extra moisture from your hair rather than rubbing it dry with a towel. Follow that up by running a wide-toothed comb through your wet locks. You should always start combing from the ends of your hair when working on getting those tangles out.

SPLIT-END SECRETS

What is a split end and why does it happen? Split ends occur when the hair shaft splits into two or three strands after the protective cuticle of the hair fiber has been stripped away. This happens to hair damaged by anything from weather to chemical processing to over-brushing.

healthy hair

split end

The best defense against split ends is keeping

your hair healthy with a trim every three months or so. This will help keep your ends from drying out and splitting. You can also use conditioner on your ends regularly for added protection.

HAIR CARE 101

∫hampoo

THERE IS A WIDE VARIETY OF SHAMPOOS on the market, but it's always best to use a mild one, especially if you wash your hair frequently. Most brands indicate whether they are for oily or dry hair. You probably know which type of hair you have, but if your hair always looks oily by the end of the day, that speaks for itself. On the other hand, curly hair tends to be dry. Here are your best bets for different types of hair:

Memo from Marlene

There are those who believe that "rinse and repeat" is a gimmick made up by the shampoo industry to get you to use twice the amount of shampoo. It's true!

OILY

- Wash your hair every morning, so it will be fresh all day. Use a mild or clear shampoo, such as baby shampoo, since you will be washing it frequently.
- Use conditioner only halfway down the hair shaft to the end.
- Massage the scalp with baking soda to soak up extra oil.
- Resist the temptation to constantly touch your hair during the day. Oils and dirt from your hands spread to your hair.

DRY

- Wash your hair only when it's dirty.
- Condition, condition, condition—every time you shampoo.
- Consider a deep-conditioning treatment once or twice a month.
- Curly hair is on the dry side and responds well to leave-in conditioners.

Fun Fact

Each person has about 100,000 hairs on his or her head.

THIN

- Use a volumizing shampoo, but beware of weighing down your hair with product.
- To avoid buildup, dilute the shampoo with water: Use a cup to measure one part shampoo to four parts water. It will get your hair just as clean without leaving a residue that can weigh down your hair.
- Use conditioner sparingly, and mostly on your ends.

THICK

- Don't think that you need more shampoo because you have more hair. Thick hair is usually porous, so the shampoo actually spreads out when rubbed onto your head.
- Use conditioner every time you shampoo.
- Rinse your hair in cold water for extra shine, since thick hair can sometimes look dull.

The Kitchen Sink

HAIR THERAPY RIGHT OUT OF YOUR FRIDGE.

Here are a few homemade hair treatments.

SOFTENING HAIR RINSE

1 tablespoon apple cider vinegar

3 cups distilled water

Mix ingredients together in a bottle and pour
over your hair as a final rinse after shampooing and conditioning. This works for all
hair types.

FOR SUMMERY BLOND HIGHLIGHTS

lemon juice

Squeeze lemon juice into a plastic spray bottle and
bring it to the beach. After swimming, spray the juice
onto your hair and let it sit for twenty minutes. Then
wash it out and rinse your hair with water. Wash
your hands immediately after using the lemon
juice—the citric acid can irritate your palms.

COMBAT CHLORINE

Especially for swimmers, this concoction will keep chlorine
from damaging your hair.

1 egg

½ cup of olive oil

¼ of a peeled cucumber

Blend all the ingredients in a blender and spread the mixture evenly throughout your hair. Leave it on for ten minutes and then rinse. Try this treatment once a month to remove the chemical residue from your hair.

HOMEMADE CONDITIONER

½ cup of mayonnaise

Apply the mayonnaise to damp hair. Work into hair and then cover with a shower cap or towel for up to twenty minutes. Rinse thoroughly and shampoo.

ANTI-FRIZZ TREATMENT

1 tablespoon of honey

1 quart of water

Mix the honey with the water for a rinse after shampooing your hair. Apply to hair and rinse out.

HAIR 911

BAD HAIR DAYS ARE PART OF LIFE. Everyone has them once in a while. Still, you can do something to combat common styling problems. Here are solutions to everyday hair emergencies.

PROBLEM: HAIR-RAISING STATIC

Solution: Rub a fabric softener sheet from the clothes dryer over your hair. It banishes static instantly.

PROBLEM: COWLICKS

Solution: Wet your cowlick and style it in place. Apply styling wax or pomade to keep it down.

PROBLEM: FRIZZ

Solution: Spray hair with a light conditioning spray and let it air dry.

33

LET'S PLAY WITH MAKEUP!

NOW THAT WE'VE CREATED THE perfect chic coif, it's time to think about our faces. A lot of little girls love to play with makeup, and maybe you were one of them, smearing your mom's lipstick all over your face.

So now we're going to experiment in a grown-up way. Proceed with caution! Remember, when it comes to makeup, a little goes a long way. Makeup products should enhance your natural beauty, not mask it. With your parents' permission, here are a few basic products to try for special occasions.

Blush

A LITTLE BIT OF COLOR ON YOUR CHEEKS is the simplest way to transform your face and give it a healthy glow. But blush can be tricky. Use too much and you'll look like a clown with bright red spots on your cheeks! Stick with light, sheer colors such as pale pinks, berry stains, and light bronzes.

COLOR CHART: BLUSH

- Pink works best on pale skin.

- Olive skin calls for berry or rose colors.

- Brown skin looks good in plum or bronze tones.

APPLICATION

The best way to apply, whether the blush is powder, cream or a stain, is to start by making a big smile so your cheeks become like little apples. Put the blush directly on the apples of your cheeks, blend a bit upward and downward, and let the glowing begin!

Memo from Marlene

When applying powder blush, blow gently on the brush before you hit your cheeks. This will make sure excess blush ends up in the sink and not on your face. It's always easier to add more blush than to take off too much.

Mascara

DARK EYELASHES ARE THE ESSENCE OF glamour. Black is the most dramatic color, but you might want to start out with brown mascara or even clear if you've never used it before. Once you have more experience, waterproof mascara is a good choice. Remember— no rubbing your eyes, no matter what kind of mascara you use!

APPLICATION

- Pull the wand out of the tube. If there is extra product clumped at the tip, carefully remove it with a tissue.

- Staring straight ahead, apply the mascara to the top set of lashes. Begin in the center, at the root of the lashes, then move the brush to the outer lashes.

- Once you are finished, bat your eyelashes against your index finger to remove any excess mascara.

- For the bottom set of lashes, hold the wand perpendicular to your eye and move it back and forth lightly against the lashes. Some models think applying mascara to the top lashes only is a cleaner, more contemporary look, but see what looks best on you.

Lip Gloss

SHEER COLORS AND LIGHT STAINS ARE THE way to go when you're first starting out. You'll look fresh and modern, and they're easy to apply. It's almost impossible to make a mistake, and you don't even have to blot your lips on a tissue! Berry colors look terrific on every smile under the sun. You can start out with a cherry-colored lip balm that will protect your pout while making it pretty. You can even get glosses that have a candy taste, so check around in the drugstore.

39

APPLICATION

Some glosses come with a wand to apply the color, but your finger works just as well as an applicator. The thicker or stickier the gloss, the less you should use. If it's a light stain, feel free to apply it across both upper and bottom lips. If you are using a shiny lip gloss, put a dab on the middle of your bottom lip and then rub your lips together.

Cheat Sheet!

IF YOU FIND YOUR LIPS ARE PEELING

or your gloss is getting clumpy, you might need to exfoliate. That's right—sometimes you need to slough off dead skin from your lips. Using your clean toothbrush, brush your lips very, very lightly, then rinse with water. If your lips are super-sensitive, you can use a washcloth instead. In either case, the result will be soft, lovely lips.

BE YOUR OWN MAKEUP ARTIST

MAKEUP ARTISTS WORK IN A variety of different settings. They work in department stores, on movie sets, and for music videos, fashion shoots, and runway shows. Others work freelance at special events.

Paula Dorf is one of the top makeup artists in the world. She has done makeup for magazine covers, feature films, and music videos, and has her own makeup line. As a little girl, Paula loved to play with her mother's makeup because she was fascinated by all the colors. "It was always my passion to become a makeup artist," says the New York City resident, who got her start by doing her friends' makeup for their Sweet Sixteen parties. She has risen to the top of her field by being a great listener. "Listening to what the person wants to look like is very important," Paula explains. "I'm fulfilled when I make other people happy." Her biggest tip is to "wear makeup that complements who you are. Don't follow trends. Aspire to set your own trends and be your own person." Now, that kind of advice suits everyone!

With three different looks, specially created by Paula, you can see what it's like to be a makeup artist. Each look—Princess, Rock Star, and Fresh-Faced—can be created using inexpensive products from your local drugstore that you're already familiar with, plus some fun eye shadow colors. This is just for fun and practice, so don't break the bank on lipsticks

and glosses. Try the different styles of makeup on yourself. Or grab a friend, or even your mom, and let the makeup artistry begin. By the time you are really ready to wear makeup, you'll be a pro.

PRINCESS

1. Start with a light brown eye shadow all over the eyelid.
2. Apply black mascara to lashes.
3. Dust a pale pink cheek color on the apples of the cheeks.
4. Finish with a bright pink lip gloss.

ROCK STAR

1. Start with a glitter eye shadow in a cream or gel all over the eyelid.

2. Choose a dark mascara and coat the upper and lower lashes.

3. Apply a pale pink cheek color to the apples of the cheeks.

4. Finish with a very shiny lip gloss with lots of glitter.

44

FREJH-FACED

1. Apply natural brown or clear mascara to lashes.

2. Dust a peachy beige or light bronzing powder on the apples of the cheeks.

3. Finish with a clear lip gloss or lip balm.

Memo from Marlene

When shopping for school supplies, sneak in an extra pencil case and turn it into a makeup bag. Don't waste time fishing around in your backpack for your favorite lip gloss. Put your lip gloss, mascara, and blush in the case for maximum organization—pop in a small mirror, too.

Make
copies
of this
page and
keep a log of
the different
looks you create.

Sketch your next makeup look!

chapter 2
SKIN DEEP

OUR BODIES HAVE LOTS OF DIFF-erent organs, and some of them need special attention. For instance, we all need to eat healthy foods and not smoke in order to take care of our hearts. Did you know your skin is the largest organ in your body? It is! You need to take special care of your skin, too. The following is essential to general good health as well as glowing skin:

- Your skin will look better if you have a diet filled with fruits, veggies, and whole grains that nourish you with plenty of vitamins.

- Regular exercise is key for skin health, because it improves blood circulation so that those nutrients are delivered to your skin.
- Drink water, water, water! Getting enough H_2O helps your skin stay hydrated and helps flush away impurities.

You will hear this advice over and over again. These are just the basics, but there is so much more to learn. Now is the time to establish good habits so that your skin will stay healthy and look beautiful.

PUT ON YOUR THINKING CAP

TAKING GOOD CARE OF YOUR SKIN IS just plain smart. But what does it mean to "take good care" of your skin? Well, it's as easy as putting on your thinking CAP (Clean, Apply, Protect). Follow these instructions and you'll get a great start to the day or night.

Clean Your Face Twice a Day

telling you to wash your face? She isn't just trying to help you stay clean. She's giving you a fundamental tip for your daily beauty routine. The basis of your entire skin regimen starts with washing your face. You should always wash it clean in the morning after you wake up and in the evening, right before

you go to bed. That helps get rid of dead skin, excess oil, and other environmental buildup. Even if you are really tired after a school dance or the longest soccer practice of your life, don't skip a quick wash.

There seem to be hundreds of face cleansers on the market, so it can be a pretty daunting task to choose one. Don't be fooled by fancy labels, big price tags, or a long list of ingredients. What you want is a mild soap or a cleanser without perfumes. Opt for a foaming or gel cleanser only if your skin is really oily, and please, please, please don't use

Got Water?

Moisturizer is all about water. If you look at the label, you'll see that water is usually the first ingredient listed. For glowing skin, you need to get hydroactive! That means filling up on water, both inside and out. Lotion alone won't do the trick. You need to drink water so your system gets moisturized. But another great way to stay hydrated is to eat raw fruits and vegetables. Why? Because they are filled with water. The structure of the water cells in fruits and vegetables is also hydrating for your skin. The H_2O that comes from raw fruits and veggies can enter the cells of your skin more easily because they have more protons than the cells in tap or bottled water. So eat up!

the same bar of soap you use on your body for your face. If your face feels tight and dry after a wash, it's a signal that the soap is too harsh.

Washing your face is pretty simple, but there's a right way *and* a wrong way. To do it correctly, start by washing your hands. How on earth will your face be clean if you wash with dirty hands? Use warm (not hot) water and apply cleanser with your hands, using a circular motion. Don't tug on your face, because that can stretch your skin, which is fragile. Dry your skin by patting your face with a towel.

Apply Moisturizer

THE BEST SKIN CARE REGIMENS ARE THE simplest ones. Despite all the products available, most teen-agers only need to wash their face with a mild cleanser and then apply a moisturizer for hydration, which means adding water to your skin. Most oily skin issues can be cleared up by washing your face twice a day (for additional skin care tips, see Weather Alert on page 64). Toners and astringents, popular with kids, can actually dry out and irri-tate the skin so much that they can *cause* acne breakouts.

To keep your skin in the right balance for beauty, moisturize, moisturize, moisturize. There are two choices: lotion and cream.

Lotion has more water in its formula, so it's lighter on the skin; cream is heavier and more intense. If your skin is on the oily side, go for a lotion and use it only before bedtime. Drier skin types should opt for a cream to use twice a day—both morning and night.

Whatever type of skin you have, put your moisturizer on right after you wash your face, when your skin is still moist. That's when your skin will really drink up the moisture.

Protect Your Skin from the Sun

PUTTING ON SUNSCREEN MIGHT BE THE last part of your beauty regimen, but it certainly isn't the least important. You're active and love to be outside, but you must make sure your skin is protected from the harmful rays of the sun every day—not just in the summer.

SPF refers to the degree to which sunscreen protects the skin from the direct rays of the sun, and it ranges from 2 to 45. You should always use a sunscreen with an SPF of 15 or more in order to get adequate

sun protection, because certain rays damaging to the skin are present regardless of the weather or how long you're outside. If you're outside for a longer period of time, use a product with at least SPF 30. Ideally, you should try to avoid direct sun between eleven a.m. and two p.m., when the sun's rays are the strongest. But that isn't always possible—especially if you play sports. So lather on the sunscreen about half an hour before going out. And don't forget to reapply it when you sweat a lot or go swimming, or if a couple of hours have passed. Sunscreen is as much about how much you use as how many times you layer it on.

Be a smart consumer when it comes to sunscreen and read the label of your sunscreen. It should provide both UVA and UVB protection. All sunlight has both ultraviolet A (UVA)

Memo from Marlene

Don't forget your sunglasses when you're out in the sun. Make sure they have UVA and UVB protection. If you are out in the intense sun, try sunglasses with polarized lenses, which reduce glare and protect your eyes.

and ultraviolet B (UVB) rays. Ultraviolet rays are the main cause of damage to the skin. UVA and UVB have different characteristics.

UVA RAYS:

- Cause long-term skin damage
- Penetrate deep into skin layers
- Can pass through window glass
- Are present in all different kinds of weather or altitude
- Are present all day, every day
- Are twenty times more abundant than UVB rays

UVB RAYS:

- Cause tanning and sunburn
- Are protected against by the sun protection factor (SPF)
- Are most intense at midday (eleven a.m. to two p.m.)
- Are related to more than 90 percent of certain types of cancer cells
- Cannot pass through window glass
- Vary by season and weather conditions

If you insist on that sun-kissed look, please keep in mind that the strongest rays of the sun are present from eleven a.m. to two p.m. and should be avoided if at all possible. It's believed that those who consistently get sunburned when they're younger are more likely to develop skin cancer cells when they're older—not to mention getting wrinkles and age spots. Think ahead—not just about getting tan.

Cheat Sheet!

SUNSCREEN IS GOOD FOR ONLY ONE year after the tube or bottle has been opened. Heat can speed up its expiration, so don't leave your sunscreen in the car or anywhere it will be exposed to high temperatures for a prolonged period. Sunscreen expires three years after it has been manufactured. There is usually an expiration date on the package.

Quiz: Fun in the Sun

Complete the following statements with UVA or UVB:

1. _____ is present when it's raining out.

2. _____ gives you the sun-kissed look.

3. _____ is protected against with sunscreen.

4. _____ is much more present than the other UV rays.

5. _____ may fade the rug in a sunroom.

6. _____ is more intense at certain times of the day.

7. _____ is highly related to cancer cells.

8. _____ does not stay on the skin's surface.

9. _____ will not fade the curtains in your living room.

10. _____ contributes to aging and skin damage.

SHINING THE LIGHT ON SUNSCREEN LIES

Here's the truth behind common myths about sun protection.

"You don't need sunscreen in the winter." Yes, you do! The sun is even stronger when it reflects off the snow.

"Bronzers or self-tanning lotions protect skin from the sun." Your skin is actually more vulnerable to sun damage twenty-four hours after you put on self-tanner. So make sure to put sunscreen over your newly (safely) bronzed color.

"You need only a thin coat of sunscreen." No, you need to use at least one-half teaspoon of sunscreen to get adequate coverage for your face. Each arm needs one-half teaspoon, one-half teaspoon for your stomach and chest, another half-teaspoon for your back, and one teaspoon for each leg. Try measuring out these quantities before you apply it so you get a sense of how much you really need.

Memo from Marlene

Whenever you apply sunscreen, you should use protection for your lips, too. The skin on your lips is very thin and burns easily, so use a lip balm with at least SPF 15 and smile, knowing you're fully protected.

"Tanning beds are a safe way to get a tan." False. Stay away from tanning salons. This is especially true for tweens, whose fast-growing cells are particularly vulnerable to the UVA and UVB radiation that comes from both the sun and tanning devices. National and world health organizations have declared that no one under eighteen should use a tanning bed.

WEATHER ALERT

YOU KNOW FROM EXPERIENCE THAT your skin feels different during different seasons. The winter's harsh winds can dry and crack your face, while the summer months make that same skin feel oily! Here's how you can look beautiful all year round.

Supple Skin in the Dead of Winter

SKIN OFTEN FEELS DRY AND ITCHY IN winter because the air outside is very dry. Heat inside buildings during the cold months can also be very drying. During the coldest months, the skin's protective layer struggles to stay hydrated. If your skin gets dried out in the winter, choose a creamy soap-free cleanser.

Limit shower time and use warm water, not hot. This way you won't strip the protective layer or the much-needed oil from your skin. Use a loofah or a salt scrub in the shower to exfoliate. After you take a bath or shower, make sure to apply lotion all over your body. Don't forget to include feet and elbows, which tend

My Notes

Hey, are you a freckle face? Don't hide. Lots of models and movie stars have freckles. The scientific name for freckles is ephelides. Freckles are clusters of pigment cells—meaning cells that have color in them. They pop up or become darker when the skin is exposed to sunlight. While they're most common on people with fair skin, just about any kind of skin can have freckles.

to get especially dry. That'll help with the itch factor. But if you find you're still all dried out, consider getting a humidifier to put some moisture back in your bedroom.

No-Shine Look for Summer

ON A HOT SUMMER DAY IT'S EASY TO FEEL like an oil slick is forming on your face. How is it possible to get that oily? The truth is, you don't actually produce more oil in the heat, but the humidity makes it feel like you do. The moisture from the air and your own sweat mixes with your natural oils to give you that greasy feeling. So keep the moisture down by opting for lotions instead of creams. Lotions feel lighter because they contain more water than cream does. A great trick for wiping away that grease is to buy little packs of facial blotting papers sold in drugstores. The blotting paper wipes away and absorbs the oil!

Clean and Green

FREQUENT BATHING IS ESSENTIAL TO GOOD personal hygiene. You already know that if you go too long without a shower or bath, no amount of perfume or deodorant will cover up the smell of sweat and body odor. For most people, it's not necessary to bathe every day. Showering every other day is usually a good rule unless you are playing sports or swimming, or if you sweat a lot. When you do hop into the shower, you may not realize it, but you have a chance to help the environment and conserve water.

- Turn off the shower while you lather your hair.
- Limit your showers to five minutes and your baths to five inches of water.
- Don't flush the toilet unnecessarily—each flush uses five to seven gallons of water. Put tissues and other trash in the wastebasket.
- Take a "Navy shower" twice a week. Wet yourself, turn the water off, lather up, turn the water on, and rinse off.

Take this quiz to see how your skin care style stacks up.

✳

1. When you open your medicine cabinet, you see:

A. dozens of different kinds of face wash, creams, and toners spilling out (1 point)

B. a lonely toothbrush and box of Band-Aids (2 points)

C. your favorite face wash, lotion, and sunscreen neatly lined up (3 points)

2. You're on vacation with your family and it's high noon. Your plan of action is to:

A. ignore the sun while you join every activity the hotel offers (2 points)

B. slather on SPF 700 and avoid the sun like the plague (1 point)

C. duck under the nearest umbrella until the sun gets lower, then head out covered in SPF 30 (3 points)

3. Before bedtime, you always:

A. write in your diary and meditate

(2 points)

B. steam your face with a warm wash-

cloth, cleanse with a foaming wash, and moisturize with a

light invigorating lotion (1 point)

C. quickly splash on some soap and water before you brush

your teeth (3 points)

4. Your idea of heaven is:

A. an afternoon of TV, junk food, and nothing else (2 points)

B. a mall packed with people and big sales (1 point)

C. hanging out with your best friends (3 points)

5. When packing a snack for a school field trip, you grab:

A. a water bottle, an apple, and a chocolate

chip cookie (3 points)

B. a can of soda and some licorice (2 points)

C. your body weight in water and so many carrots you might

turn orange (1 point)

6. When you get a pimple, here's what you do:

A. ignore it and let nature take its course (2 points)

B. unveil an array of sterilized surgical instruments and go to town picking the pimple (1 point)

C. apply some pimple medicine and forget about it (3 points)

7. The color that best describes you is:

A. sky blue (3 points)

B. shocking pink (1 point)

C. silver (2 points)

8. If you could choose any beauty treatment, you would pick:

A. a three-hour facial and a hot stone massage (1 point)

B. a cute manicure-pedicure (3 points)

C. You would rather skip it and read the fun magazines while waiting for your friends. (2 points)

9. Your mom is always bugging you to:

A. let loose a little and try a different hairstyle from your usual ponytail (3 points)

B. brush your hair *and* your teeth (2 points)

C. stop diving into her creams, perfumes, and face products (1 point)

10. Your fantasy profession is:

A. rock star (1 point)

B. chef (2 points)

C. veterinarian (3 points)

If you had . . .

10–17 points:

YOU LIKE TO TAKE WHATEVER YOU DO TO THE MAX— and that includes your beauty routine. Whether it's a four-hour morning ritual that involves layers and layers of cream or a desire to get a deep tan as soon as the warm weather hits, you enthusiastically embrace anything you believe will improve your appearance. You need to watch out that you don't get sucked in by fads or ads.

18–24 points:

BRONZER. TONER. LOOFAH. THESE TERMS MAY WELL BE Greek for all you know. You have a lot of interests, but exfoliating isn't one of them. You're lucky if you can muster up the energy it takes to wash your face before you go to bed. Okay, it's great that you aren't obsessed with your looks, but caring for your skin is critical. It's a health issue as well as a beauty issue. That's especially true when it comes to using sunscreen. Sun damage, even at an early age, can cause skin cancer later on. Set up a simple skin care routine that you can stick to.

25–30 points:

YOU'RE A THREE-SQUARE-MEAL KIND OF GIRL. AND YOUR beverage of choice? Water, naturally. Your approach to skin care is equally balanced. You know it's important to wash your face twice a day and keep your skin hydrated with moisturizer. Keep up the good work, but don't give yourself a hard time if you miss a spot of SPF. Nobody's perfect.

DR. HOWARD MURAD IS A

world-famous dermatologist who teaches at the University of Southern California in Los Angeles and founded his own skin care company, Murad Inc. Dr. Murad, who treats patients with all kinds of skin problems and has been interviewed in many magazines and on television, says that when it comes to skin care, "It is never too early and it is never too late to get started." Listening to what he has to say is definitely a great beginning.

Why did you want to become a dermatologist?

I HAD HORRIBLE ACNE WHEN I WAS A KID. MY FACE WAS ONE big pimple. It bothered me and lowered my self-esteem. I was shy. When I went to med school, I didn't know what kind of doctor I wanted to be. But as the years went on, I decided on dermatology. I wanted to help people with bad skin problems like I had when I was a kid.

What does a dermatologist do?

WE TREAT SKIN DISEASES, LIKE ECZEMA, AND ALSO HELP improve the appearance of people's skin. I choose to treat skin holistically by encouraging a better diet. It is more advantageous in the long run than a Botox shot. The skin is connected to the whole body. If we can help the skin, we can help the body.

What is your favorite part of your job?

MY FAVORITE PART IS TREATING PATIENTS. I CAN SEE THE results of my work on the skin. Seeing a patient have her skin clear up satisfies me—I have done something really good in life.

When should a girl start taking care of her skin?

IF YOU START WITH GOOD HABITS EARLY ON, IT IS EASIER to maintain rather than trying to change your habits later. The sooner you start, the better.

What's a common mistake kids make when it comes to their skin?

DON'T PICK A PIMPLE, BECAUSE YOU CAN CAUSE SCARRING. If you have to do something, put a warm towel on your face, allow the pustule to come to a head, and just gently squeeze it, using tissues, instead of digging at it with your bare fingers. Clean hands are a MUST!

What should people do about acne?

THE INTAKE OF VARIOUS NUTRIENTS CAN MAKE A BIG difference with acne. People should eat zinc, which is found in a lot of nuts and seeds, drink chamomile tea, and take vitamin A, which is in yellow vegetables. Acne is an inflammatory disease. If we reduce the inflammation, we reduce the red bumps. You can apply cucumbers to pimples because they take away the inflammation and are hydrating. With acne you don't want to dry out your skin, just reduce the redness.

What advice would you give kids about their skin?

IT'S NORMAL TO HAVE SOME IMPERFECTIONS. DON'T DWELL on them. Most people don't even see what you are focusing

on. If need be, get a facial and then feel good about yourself. Why have a bad day when you can have a good day?
Try to look at the positive.

Memo
from Marlene

Wonder what Dr. Murad
would say about using toothpaste to dry up a pimple?
He'd probably say it was okay in
a pinch. But no one would say
it's okay to pick at
a pimple!

chapter 3
THE REST OF YOU

DO YOU KNOW WHAT IT MEANS TO be manicured? No, it's not something that happens only to your nails. The real definition is someone who has personal polish, from head to toe. It has everything to do with attitude and energy, and nothing to do with inherited traits such as a model's high cheekbones or long legs. Personal style and good grooming are a matter of creating your own health and beauty routines. Your style is easy to achieve if you put a little effort into it, and after a while it becomes a no-brainer. You will be amazed at the overall results. A manicured girl is someone who pays attention to all the details—clean hands, healthy feet, sparkling teeth, fresh scent—for a look that always impresses. And yes, a lifestyle with personal polish may include an actual manicure, so let's start there.

STUNNING HANDS

How to Create Beautiful Hands

THE FIRST STEP TO LOVELY HANDS IS THE bar of soap on your sink. Washing your hands is crucial to a healthy lifestyle, since your hands come in contact with a lot of germs throughout your day. In order to prevent getting colds and flus, you need to scrub your hands to get rid of bacteria you've picked up. That means a thorough washing, in which you lather up each hand to the wrist for at least thirty seconds and then rinse off under running water. You should wash your hands whenever you use the bathroom and before you eat.

All this washing can easily dry out your hands. Use hand cream to keep your mitts from cracking. You can never use too much hand cream, and the thicker the better, especially before bedtime. You might want to keep a bottle of cream next to your bed so you can put it on when you are doing homework, reading a magazine, before you go to sleep, or whenever you think of it.

The number one reason for hangnails is dry cuticles, which result from dry hands. It's important not to pick at or bite your cuticles. And don't cut them; they can easily get infected. The cuticle functions as a barrier between the nail and the skin on your finger. It keeps bacteria from entering your body, so you don't want to destroy that barrier. That doesn't mean you can't groom them. In order to get a nice big nail bed with neat cuticles, after a shower or bath push them back from the nail bed gently with a wet washcloth.

Afterward, just dab a drop of cuticle cream or oil on your cuticle and massage it in. That's a simple way to maintain nice-looking cuticles.

For rosy, healthy nails, be sure you get enough zinc and iron in your diet. Zinc can be found in nuts, seeds, poultry, and whole grains. There's a lot of iron in red meat and beans. These minerals will help you grow thicker nails. Brittle nails break easily. And avoid acetone-based polish removers, because they dry out nails.

How to Give Yourself a Basic Manicure

MANICURES ARE EASY TO DO AND QUICKLY improve your appearance. You can give yourself one in minutes and save the money you would spend in the salon. The more manicures you do, the better you'll get at it.

Here's what you'll need:

- Nail clippers
- Fine-grade nail file
- Hand cream
- Clear nail polish
- Colored nail polish
- Orangewood stick (Commonly called an orange stick, this is a thin stick with a pointed end for cleaning nails and a rounded end to push back cuticles; you can get it at any drugstore.)
- Cotton balls
- Tissue

The first step to a fabulous manicure is clean hands, so wash up. Next, take an orangewood stick, wrap a piece of the cotton ball tightly around it, and clean any dirt under your fingernails.

Clip your nails, moving from one side of the nail to the other in a U-shape around your finger (that shape makes your nails appear longer). If possible, make all your nails the same length.

Take the nail file and sweep it over the edge of each nail a few times to smooth it out.

Massage the cream into your hands and nails. Rub your cuticles with some cream too, especially if they're dry. Wipe the excess moisturizer off with a tissue.

Paint your nails with a clear polish (called the base coat) and give it a few minutes to dry. Then apply two coats of colored nail polish. Finish off with another coat of clear polish (called a top coat). Make sure you rest the palm of the hand that's doing the painting on a surface to steady it. Let your nails dry for at least twenty minutes before you use your hands so you won't smudge your beautiful manicure. You have four coats of polish on, so you need to let it dry!

Once the polish seems dry, take the orangewood stick, wrapped with a piece of cotton ball dipped in nail polish

84

remover, and clean off any excess polish around your finger-nails. Be careful to wrap the cotton ball tightly so the little fibers don't end up stuck in the polish.

Stop Biting Those Nails!

NAIL BITING IS A BAD HABIT IN SO MANY ways. For one, it's dirty. As you already know, your hands come in contact with millions of germs every day. So sticking them into your mouth is a surefire way to get sick. Also, the ragged edges created by gnawing at your nails are as far from the manicured look as possible. Last, when people catch you nibbling on your fingers, you look insecure and scared. That's not who you are, so follow the tips below to quit that bad habit.

- Clip your nails so short that there is nothing to bite.
- Cover your nails with pretty gloves until you break the habit.

Fun Fact
Your nails grow faster in warm weather because blood flow, which stimulates growth, is increased in warmer temperatures.

- Use a treatment on your nails that makes them taste bitter so you won't want to bite.

FABULOUS FEET

YOUR FEET TAKE A LOT OF ABUSE. You try to wear comfortable shoes, but occasionally you make your tootsies suffer for fashion. It's easy for your feet to run into problems. Here are solutions to the most common foot troubles.

- To prevent ingrown toenails, make sure to cut your toenails straight across. Never rip your nails with your fingers. If you think you may have an ingrown toenail, soak it in water with Epsom salts and wear wide shoes. If you think there's an infection, let your parents know.

- Wearing nail polish on your toes for extended periods of time can turn your nails yellow. Give your toes a breather from polish every now and then. Soak your nails in lemon juice to return them to their original color. When you use nail polish, look for a variety that comes in a non-yellowing formula.

- Everyone gets blisters sometimes, but you should absolutely resist the temptation to pop them, as this can cause an infection. Apply antibiotic ointment to the blister and cover it with a bandage so your shoes won't rub the tender area. Even in the summer, it's best if you can wear socks for a couple of days.

Memo from Marlene

If you are like me, when you buy a cute pair of shoes, you want to wear them until the soles fall off. Please don't do it! If you wear the same shoes day after day, they will rub your feet over and over in the same spot, which can cause blisters and calluses. To reduce the rubbing, apply petroleum jelly anywhere you feel irritation. Rotating your footwear helps to ensure that different pressure points get targeted so you don't wind up with blisters. Even shoes that are comfortable may hurt if you wear them all the time.

HOW TO FLASH THE PERFECT SMILE

YOUR SMILE IS YOUR CALLING CARD. The way you smile can really influence what people think of you when they meet you for the first time. There is a famous model who is known for her repertoire of smiles—275 in all, from the surprise smile to the flirty smile to the smile with the eyes only.She spent a lot of time in front of the mirror perfecting her hundreds of smiles. You should try to do the same. Stand in front of the mirror and experiment with different smiles. Even if you have just a few smiles, they'll make you seem more expressive and dynamic.

Dental Hygiene

IF YOU DON'T TAKE CARE OF YOUR TEETH, you'll end up jeopardizing the smile you worked so hard to perfect. Think you already know everything there is to know about dental care? There's more to it than you realize. Read on to find out more.

88

Bracing for Trouble

your teeth—brushing and flossing every day and not eating too many sweets—you may still need some extra help with your smile. That's right, straightening your teeth. Braces will do the trick. The process starts with a visit to the orthodontist, a dentist who specializes in straightening teeth. The orthodontist will examine your mouth and suggest one of a few types of braces, or "appliances," as the pros call them. These devices are designed to stabilize the teeth and jaw. Braces

do more than straighten your teeth, however. They also help create a healthy bite, which protects against tooth decay. Straight teeth are a nice bonus. Braces have come a long way—check out the options.

Braces can be either fixed or removable. While the removable kind, sometimes called retainers, are usually used to hold straightened teeth in their new place, fixed braces are used to correct crooked teeth or an overbite. On fixed braces, the combination of brackets, bands, and wires are attached to your teeth by the orthodontist using special tools. Adults as well as teens may have to wear braces, and they often need to keep them on for a year or longer. There are several styles to choose from; talk with your orthodontist about which of the following is right for you.

Metal braces: This the most common type, and they've been around the longest. Metal braces are usually made of stainless steel, but you can even order them in gold. They tend to be the most affordable option, but they are also the most visible.

Ceramic braces: These braces are either clear or tooth-colored, so they are less visible than metal ones. Aside from being nearly invisible, ceramic braces are less likely to leave stain marks on your teeth. They are more expensive than most metal braces, and you may need to wear them longer.

Lingual braces: These braces are attached to the insides of the teeth. That makes them totally invisible, but they can cut

the inside of the mouth and make it harder to talk. Lingual braces are often used in the short term, to hold the jaw in place while one or more teeth are removed.

What About Tooth Whiteners?

PLEASE CONSULT WITH YOUR DENTIST BEFORE using any whitener, even whitening toothpaste, which can wear down the enamel on your teeth with regular use. A program of daily brushing and flossing, along with regular visits to the dentist, is the best way to keep your pearly whites sparkling. Should you and your dentist decide you're able to do some whitening, there are products you can buy at the pharmacy or drugstore to help. Over-the-counter whiteners are basically superstrong toothpastes that you either brush on before you go to bed or apply for thirty minutes during the day or overnight. While the products have been proven to brighten teeth, they can irritate your gums, so you should use them sparingly, maybe once or twice a year at most and always under your dentist's supervision.

True or False?

❄

1. You should brush your tongue as well as your teeth.

T   F

2. Flossing should be done once a week.

T   F

3. It's okay to use the same toothbrush for one year.

T   F

4. The most important ingredient in toothpaste is mint.

T   F

5. You should brush your teeth for two to three minutes at least twice a day.

T   F

1. True. Bacteria hang out on the surface of the tongue, causing bad breath. 2. False. You should floss at least twice a day to remove bacteria between teeth where your toothbrush can't reach. 3. False. You need to change your toothbrush every three or four months. Don't wait until it becomes a bristle monster. And make sure to close the lid of the toilet when you flush if your toothbrush sits out on your sink. Toilet water can spray as far as six feet when you flush, so you might have the same water on your brush that you do in the toilet. Yuck! 4. False. Fluoride is the most important ingredient, because it protects against cavities. 5. True. When you brush, you need to clean every surface on every tooth, and that takes time. Most people think they brush for long enough, but they actually brush for thirty seconds or less. If you sing your favorite song in your head while brushing, you won't fall into this trap.

IT MAKES SCENTS

PERFUMERY, OR THE ART OF MAKING aromatic potions for the body, has been around since ancient times. During the Renaissance, between the fourteenth and seventeenth centuries, perfumes were worn by royalty as a way to mask body odor. Today we have deodorants for that, but perfume is as popular as ever. Wearing a fragrance is an excellent way to express a

Memo from Marlene

Buyer beware: "Natural," "botanical," "organic," and "herbal" are all terms used to describe beauty and health products. But remember, a snakebite is natural, and poison ivy is botanical. Natural products are not necessarily safer or more effective. Consult a healthcare professional, and be an educated consumer about the products you purchase.

particular mood. For example, some perfumes smell like a spring day after a rainfall, evoking an easygoing spirit that might be just right for a casual lunch with friends. Other fragrances are more sophisticated, with rich floral notes that might be better saved for a special occasion, such as a dance.

Finding Your Perfect Fragrance

FRAGRANCE IS VERY PERSONAL, PROBABLY because it has strong associations with memories. Maybe there was a lilac bush outside the window where you slept as a baby. You don't remember the bush, but the smell of

lilac is locked in your memory bank. This is why finding the perfect perfume is a very special process. Just because a scent smells great on your best friend doesn't mean it will be right for you, because fragrance mixes with your own unique personal scent. Try on lots of scents. (But not at the same time!) See which ones you think smell sweet—or just stink. Make sure you wear a perfume for at least a couple of hours before you buy it, since the scent will change as it mingles with your skin. It's fun to get some samples at the perfume counter in department stores. You can even start a collection with the mini bottles.

Smelling Sweet

ONCE YOU FINALLY FIND YOUR SIGNATURE scent, you'll want to be sure to put it on properly. The rule of thumb is to apply the fragrance where your skin is the warmest. The most common pulse points are behind the ears, on the wrist, just below the neck, along the clavicle (that bone just above the chest), and behind the knees.

Memo from Marlene

You may want to try a scent for a few days to see if it works for you. You can often get free samples at makeup counters.

- Apply some unscented baby oil or petroleum jelly where you put the perfume. It will give the perfume something to cling to.
- Spray perfume on your clothes as well as your pulse points.
- Spray perfume on your hair, which easily absorbs odors and keeps them until your next shampoo.

A big problem with a lot of perfumes is that they seem to evaporate quickly. Here are a few tricks to keep you smelling nice throughout the day and night.

DO-IT-YOURSELF SPA!

ALMOST EVERY CULTURE IN THE world has its own version of a spa. Having a special place to experience a day of health and beauty treatments goes all the way back to ancient times. In 25 BC, Emperor Agrippa opened the first large public baths with steam rooms in Rome. It was an instant hit. The history of the spa is so long because it's such an enjoyable experience. Who doesn't love a day of pampering? The problem is, there is often a high price tag attached. The tab for massages and mud masks can quickly add up. But you don't need a large bank account to treat yourself to a spa afternoon at your house. With your parents' permission, this is an awesome activity your friends will never forget. Let the beauty treatments begin!

Set the Scene

THE FIRST STEP IN MAKING YOUR SPA DAY is creating a relaxing environment. Who wants to put on a face mask when someone's hammering in the background? Set the scene by clearing a space in your bedroom or the living room. Put down an old sheet or two so you don't have to worry about messing up the rug with your beauty treatments. Grab fluffy pillows and put them on the sheet for maximum lounging.

Welcome to the Salon

Light a few candles and put them in the corners of the room to add to your mellow ambience. Always ask your parents first before you use candles, since they can create a fire hazard. Make sure any candles are far away from pillows, papers, or any other flammable material. Never leave a room with candles burning.

Put the finishing touches on your home spa by choosing some soft tunes that will provide a soothing backdrop. Acoustic or instrumental music are good choices. Spread out your favorite magazines on the sheet for friends to flip through while hanging out.

Treats to Eat

MOST FANCY SPAS HAVE MENUS WITH LIGHT fare to offer their customers. Hey, getting beautiful can make a girl hungry! With your parents' help, whip up fun, healthy food for your friends with these easy recipes.

APPLE BAR

apples cut into quarters

popsicle sticks

plain or vanilla yogurt

healthy toppings of your choice,

> such as shredded coconut,

> nuts, dried cranberries, or granola

Put the apple quarters onto the popsicle sticks and lay them out on a tray. Assemble the yogurt and toppings in separate bowls and line them up next to the apples. Let your guests dip the apples into the yogurt and then the toppings of their choice.

FRUIT KEBABS

fruit (pineapple, melon, berries, or

> anything you like that will

> hold its shape and not turn

> brown), cut up into cubes

wooden kebab sticks

fruit-flavored yogurt (optional)

Stack the cubed fruit on the kebab sticks. Try different combinations for a colorful and healthy treat. Use the fruit-flavored yogurt as a dipping sauce.

bread

cucumbers

cream cheese

CUCUMBER SANDWICHES

thinly sliced cucumbers

whole wheat bread with the crusts trimmed off

cream cheese

Spread a thin layer of cream cheese on the wheat bread and top with the cucumber slices. Serve the sandwiches open-faced for a little extra panache!

Prep for Beauty Treatments

HOMEMADE FACIALS ARE A FUN AND inexpensive beauty treatment to try out with friends. Before you or any of your guests apply a mask, make sure to try it out on the inside of your wrist to make sure you won't have an allergic reaction to the ingredients. Here's how to apply all the masks: Everyone should wash their faces first to get rid of lotion or any other products. After drying with a towel, apply the mask to the entire face. Make sure to keep the mixture away from the eyes, since some ingredients can cause irritation. Leave the mask on for ten minutes, rinse, and then apply moisturizer. Have a bottle of light lotion ready for your guests to apply after their masks.

Now that you know the basics, here are some easy homemade mask recipes to try. Be sure to ask your parents for help.

Fun Fact

Aromatherapy is a New Age therapy that uses essential oils from certain plants for relaxation and stress reduction. These oils are believed to affect our moods, emotions, and memory. It is said that we have the ability to distinguish ten thousand different smells.

ENERGIZING ENZYME MASK

The enzymes in pumpkin and papaya gently exfoliate skin to leave it glowing and fresh.

²/₃ cup fresh mashed papaya (scoop out the seeds)

15 ounces canned pure pumpkin

1 beaten egg

Combine the mashed papaya, beaten egg, and pumpkin, and mix the ingredients in a food processor or blender until smooth. Follow the directions above to apply.

RICH LADY MASK

This rich mask is so easy, and it will leave even the driest skin super-hydrated.

1 tablespoon yogurt

1 tablespoon honey

Mix the two ingredients in a bowl.

Follow the directions above

to apply.

104

EGG WHITE MASK

This is as simple as it gets for wonderful, fresh, smooth-feeling skin.

2 egg whites

Separate two egg whites from their yolks and put them in a bowl. Dip your hands in and massage the whites on your face in a circular motion, avoiding the eye area. Remove after fifteen minutes or when the mask "hardens." Wash off with warm water and pat dry.

Nail Detail

NO SPA DAY IS COMPLETE WITHOUT A MANI-cure. Kick your nails up a notch with fun colors and accessories that will dazzle your friends. Maybe even some nail art. Go to the drugstore and pick out a few inexpensive but wild colors such as bright pink, deep purple, even green. Metallics are great for experimenting. You should also pick up a little nail glue to apply fun items such as sequins and stickers. Also get some glitter to shake over wet nail polish for a sparkling set of hands. Encourage your friends to go wild and get really creative with their nails. Make sure to have enough polish remover and cotton balls for mistakes.

ONE-STOP SHOPPING

LIVE OIL, WHICH CAN BE FOUND in nearly every kitchen, has been the secret of Mediterranean beauties for centuries. It helps maintain good health and should be a regular part of your diet to maintain a fresh, dewy complexion and lustrous hair.

Cuticles and nails: For ragged, brittle, and dry nails, soak nails for thirty minutes in a small cup of olive oil.

Hands: For chapped hands, smooth one tablespoon of olive oil onto each hand before bed. Then put on plastic medical gloves and go to sleep. You will not believe the difference in the morning!

Lips: To soothe and heal chapped lips, dab on a little olive oil and massage one lip against the other.

Hair treatment: To make your hair shiny and silky and repair split ends, put three tablespoons of olive oil into a half cup of water. Massage the mixture into your scalp and hair. Cover hair with a plastic shower cap and leave on for thirty minutes, and then use a small amount of shampoo to wash out the oil. To help repair heat damage, you can create a more intense treatment by leaving the mixture on overnight.

Skin: To help smooth dry elbows and heels, or wherever you need softening and moisturizing, massage a small amount of olive oil into your skin. While your bathwater is running, add four tablespoons of olive oil to smooth and nourish the rest of your skin. Soak for a little while, and when you get out of the bath, massage all the residue into your skin.

chapter 4

JUST ASK MARLENE

NOW YOU KNOW THE DIFFERENCE between your cuticles and your follicles, and how to take care of both and everything in between! But that doesn't mean there isn't more to know. Whenever the models I work with have questions about health or beauty, they always say, "JAM!"—or Just Ask Marlene! That's because I always have the answers. Here are a few of their questions I've decided to share with you. Send in your own questions for Marlene at JustAskMarlene.com.

JUST ASK MARLENE ®

I love to curl my hair for special occasions, but my hair is thin and always falls flat about ten minutes after I've styled it. How can I get my curls to stay curled?

—Amy

MANY OF MY MODELS WITH STRAIGHT HAIR are faced with this problem during long days on a photo shoot, where they have to maintain their curls. It may sound strange, but some hairstyles work better if your hair is a little dirty. Try curling your hair a day or two after you've washed it. Make sure the pieces of hair you wrap around the curling iron are relatively small so that all the hair gets heated. When you are done with each section, lightly spray the curls with a medium-hold hairspray. Those curls should be bouncing all day—and night!

Whenever I go to the beach or the pool, I put on sunscreen, but I still wind up with a splotchy tan and areas where I'm burned. What's the best way to put on sunscreen so it's even all over my body?

—Kara

THERE'S NOTHING WORSE THAN WINDING up with a big red patch on your arm or thigh after a day in the sun. I've discovered a simple method to help make sure my suntan is even. Half an hour before heading out, apply sunscreen in the privacy of your own room, before you put on your bathing suit. Put it on in a methodical way—first arms, then legs, face, etc.—so you don't forget a single area. You'll have to ask for help with your back, since you can't reach. But choose carefully. You want someone who will take as much care with your sunscreen as you do. Another idea: Spray-on sunscreen can be a good way to make sure you get an even application, which means an even, and safe, tan.

I hate the mole on my cheek! It's the first thing I see when I look in the mirror. My doctor says it's not dangerous. And my mom says it's not ugly, so I can't have it removed. What should I do?

—Sienna

FIRST OF ALL, STOP CALLING IT A MOLE. IT'S A beauty mark. There's a supermodel who turned her beauty mark into a million-dollar calling card. She could have had it removed or covered it over with pancake makeup; instead she decided to use it to stand out from the crowd—in a good way. What can you do with your beauty mark? If your mother says it isn't ugly, try to see it through her eyes. Next time you look in the mirror, make yourself name all the elements of your face that you like—you might be surprised by what you say. When you're older, you can consider having it removed, but that is a conversation to have with your parents after you've really thought about it.

Test your knowledge!

✳

1. When washing your hair, do you need to rinse and repeat?

2. What are the different face types to consider when getting a haircut?

3. How many times should you wash your face each day?

4. What's the number one cause of hangnails?

5. What's the best way to care for your teeth?

6. Where's the best place to apply perfume?

1. No, unless your hair is extremely dirty—for example, if you went swimming in a murky lake. Otherwise, one washing with a quarter-size amount of shampoo is enough. 2. Round, oval, square, and heart-shaped. Figure out which one you are to determine which hairstyles will work best for you. 3. At least twice a day—in the morning and in the evening. Follow with moisturizer and sunscreen if you are headed outside. 4. Dry cuticles are usually the culprit. Fight hangnails before they arise by keeping hands constantly moisturized with cream. No picking at them, please. 5. To maintain your beautiful smile, brush twice a day with fluoride toothpaste and floss your teeth. Avoiding sugary snacks is also a good idea. 6. Scent is most fragrant on the warmest parts of the body—the pulse points, behind the ears, on the wrist, below the neck, along the clavicle, and behind the knees.

epilogue

NOW THAT YOU'VE REACHED THE end of the book, if you've learned nothing else, I hope you've learned that *beauty is only skin deep*. If you haven't learned that, please go back to page one and start reading all over again! Either way, as you get older and you have more grown-up feelings, just remember always to be the special, beautiful person you are from the inside out.

Check out the
**Behind the
Scenes at the JAM
Photo Shoot**
video online!
JustAskMarlene.com

ACKNOWLEDGMENTS

T WAS A SUMMER LUNCH WITH BARBARA Marcus, my friend and agent, where we conceived of the books. If it weren't for Barbara and the need to eat, these books would not have been written. The team at Simon & Schuster led by my editor, Emily Lawrence, helped me create what I believe will be classic lifestyle guides for young teens for years to come. Gloria Norwich and Judy Gitenstein are the special people who always made certain my voice sang throughout. The photographer, Anna Palma, along with my models from Wilhelmina Kids & Teens, helped make the images in my head a beautiful reality. And then, of course, there's my sister, Maxine Bessin, who gave me perspective along the way, just as she always has. During this process, I have realized that the collection has become the most meaningful thing in my career, as I hope that the words on these pages will make the sometimes complex adolescent experience just a little more enjoyable.

Read these books by

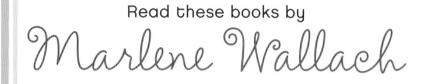

Marlene Wallach

marlene wallach
president, wilhelmina kids & teens modeling agency

My Beauty
a guide to looking
& feeling great

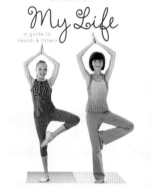

marlene wallach
president, wilhelmina kids & teens modeling agency

My Life
a guide to
health & fitness

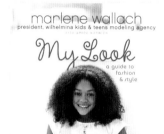

marlene wallach
president, wilhelmina kids & teens modeling agency

My Look
a guide to
fashion
& style

marlene wallach
president, wilhelmina kids & teens modeling agency

My Self
a guide
to me

Collect them all!

Amazing, crazy, wild and wonderful. Being a girl is all that and a lot more. Every day brings something new. Friends. Family. School. Sports. Hobbies. Clothes. Make-up... Boys!!! Jam wants to know what's happening with you.

Here at jam you become part of a huge community of girls from around the world who can't wait to share everything about their lives and learn about you. And where else will you be able to get the inside scoop and greatest and latest tips on

modeling • fashion • **beauty** • fitness • **self-esteem** • **fun**

This is an incredible time to be a girl. Never before have there been so many exciting activities, cool ideas, and magical possibilities.

Let's go for it! Come celebrate yourself at jam.

www.justaskmarlene.com